How to LLC

and why bother

The little book that will save your a**

How you, too, can use America's stealth business weapon!

by S. Ralf Carter

A **Grazing Rock** publication

Table of Contents

Is it important?

Seriously – why would you bother to waste your time on this work of a probably bored and untalented author?

To this question I shall respond – as every good hypocrite does – with some counter-questions:

Do you wish to lose all your property and belongings to a frivolous lawsuit, or would you rather hand it over to the IRS?

Are you self-employed, and every look at your annual tax return feels like you are giving half of your labor to the IRS?

And by far the most important question: **do you want** your business to ever, **ever** be able to work without yourself doing all the work – and it therefore be anything more than just another type of job you, the owner?

If you have answered "yes" to the first question and "no" to the other two – well, then this book is not for you. Sorry about that; our paths will be parting right here, and I wish you best luck – because you will need it.

If, however, you are still reading, then maybe there actually is some value you will have gained from the book in the end. Feel welcome in my little kingdom!

A disclaimer is necessary:

This book discusses aspects of businesses and LLCs mostly on the US federal level; some individual cases of state specialties are mentioned, but the multitude of states and municipalities would easily exceed the abilities of this book, if I were to attempt a discussion of details for each state and every city. Fortunately, the big picture is similar for all of them – for specific details in your situation and your jurisdiction, please get in touch with your attorney or accountant (whoever is the appropriate partner).

The Truth, and Nothing But

You know those nights, when the full moon is enchanting everything below it on our earth. On some days, we even recognize how bright and large the disc in the sky appears to us. How do we talk about that?

We say things like "The moon is very bright tonight" or "The moon is huge today". And everybody knows what we mean to say.

But, truth be told, those statements are plain lies. The moon is not bright at all, it isn't even an own source of light. It just reflects the sunlight or radiates the light of the creator, depending on your belief system. Or whatever else you believe to be true about the moonlight. But I haven't found anybody who really thinks the light is created by the moon itself.

Nevertheless, we plainly state that the moon IS bright. And we know it's not true. So, we are lying.

Same holds true for the statement about the moon being larger than normal. Of course, that's not really true – and yes, again, we also know that fact. So again, a lie.

Do we feel bad about saying something like "the moon is large"? No, not at all. We can do so because we know full well that everybody else is aware of the real facts behind that sentence.

Whoever is listening to us knows that we are simplifying. We are wrapping up a whole bunch of reality in a simple phrase, which allows us to make the point we want to make. Because, let's face it: the way the moon is borrowing somebody else's glamor to appear the way it does, this way doesn't change. It always works the way it does today. Just today, the result is impressing us more than usual. And **that** was the thing we really wanted to say.

So, it is generally accepted to lie – as long as everybody understands we are using a substantial simplification.

And that, dear reader, is what I will be doing throughout this book, too. Nobody really cares about the details contained in thousands and thousands of pages which make up the Internal Revenue Code (aka the "tax law"). Much less about the additional pages in the states' laws dealing with business and commerce. For most part, it is sufficient to understand to basics behind all of that – for everything else, there are experts.

Use the Experts!

People like accountants, bookkeepers, business attorneys – all of them are dealing with extremely complex matters. And that's good – because you can simply hire them and have them work on your case. Keeps you out of the legal books and in your business instead. Just pay them a sizeable amount for a short time, so your head can make more money in your own business.

By no means is this book intended to replace any of the professionals – quite the opposite. In order to work with a professional such as an attorney or an accountant, you need to know the fundamentals, else it will be hard to ask the right questions or say the right things.

In some cases, the professionals are even legally prohibited from giving you certain types of advice if they have to assume you wouldn't be able to understand it or follow through with all aspects of it. Let me repeat that: if your paid professionals have the impression you wouldn't understand certain types of advice, they are legally prohibited from giving you such advice.

Got that? That simply means: if you want to play with the big dogs, you first need to learn how to bark like one.

So – now bark!

Fine, so you won't bark for me. That's ok, you still have some time until the end of this book. But I **will** come back to it, that's a promise!

The Bottom Line

Before we dive right into the middle of the book, I want to make sure we are on somewhat the same page with our terms.

I have spent hours talking with business owners, just to find out afterwards that they have no clue what I was talking about – because they didn't know even the basics of their business financials.

So, let's try to make this very short – just enough so we don't confuse each other.

When your business is selling items or services, it will ask to be paid. The total of all those amounts for your goods and services is called **revenue** (sometimes **turnover**). So, revenue simply means the total amount of money which should be coming in.

As we all know, there is a difference between "should" and "does". While revenue tells us how much should be coming in, **cash received** tells us how much really **did** come in.

You are still with me, I hope? Let's try that right away:

I have a juicy apple and I am selling it to you for $5. But you don't have the cash with you, so you promise to pay me by tomorrow.

How much is my revenue?

I sold the apple for $5, so that amount is my revenue.

How much is my cash received?

Umm... none. You didn't pay me so far, so my cash received is zero.

Good – it looks like we are clear about those two.

Right now, you have the apple – but what do I have? I don't have the apple anymore and I don't have your payment yet. What is it that I have meanwhile?

That's called a **receivable** – because I kind of expect the amount of $5 to be received by tomorrow.

Now we know I hold a receivable, and you are holding the apple. That doesn't tell us an awful lot about my business, does it?

So, let's dig a bit deeper. I have purchased this apple an hour ago at the grocery store down the street – I have been walking over there and back, and I purchased the apple in the store for $2. Those $2 are the **cost of goods sold** – because that's pretty much what they are: the costs of the goods that I sold. Right now, it's only one item (the apple), so the cost of goods sold runs at $2. By the way, the term "cost of goods sold" is used so often that it's commonly abbreviated as **COGS**.

Why did you buy the apple from me? Well, maybe because I have a little flag saying "Apples for sale"? That probably had something to do with it, right?

This flag has cost me $1 - and somehow, I should include that in my calculation.

That's what we do right now:

My revenue was $5. Of those $5, I had to pay $2 as COGS to the store. If I subtract the COGS out of the revenue, I get the **gross margin**. That's the simple difference between revenue and COGS.

If I further subtract my general, administrative and marketing costs from the gross margin – in my case the $1 for the advertising flag – then I will get to the **income** (often also called **profit**).

As of right now, I seem to have income of $2 from revenue of $5 (because revenue minus cogs minus marketing equals income). That sounds fairly good. Just one tiny problem: I don't have any money.

That's because there was no cash received. But I did spend $2 earlier at the grocery store. To see how my cash changed over this day, I subtract **cash paid** from **cash received**: $0

(I didn't receive any cash) minus $2 (payment to the grocery store). The result is negative $2. That would kind of explain why I have so little money.

The difference between **cash received** and **cash paid** is called **cash flow**. Cash flow can be positive – then you have more cash afterwards than you had before. Or it can be negative – then you have less cash afterwards. Today clearly seems to be a day with **negative cash flow**, sometimes also called **cash flow loss**.

First lesson for business owners: don't let negative cash flow days appear too often.

At this point, it's important to notice: yes, I did indeed make a profit today. But I am cash flow negative nevertheless.

Can I use the receivable to buy another apple today? No, I cannot. Only cash will do the trick. Here you have it: neither revenue nor income allow you to pay for anything; both are just creatures of mathematics. Only positive cash flow is real and can pay for stuff. That's why cash flow deserves an own chapter, which of course you will find in this book.

Now that we have briefly looked at what we have – let me ask you:

I just found some guys on the internet who boasted about having "made $500,000 in 30 days". What are those guys talking about? Was that revenue, cash flow, profits?

They won't tell you. If nobody wants to tell you, you can safely assume it's the most useless number of all: revenue.

Why is revenue so useless for information purposes?

It's useless by itself, if not accompanied by any cash flow or income numbers. Because I can easily produce millions of dollars as revenue all day long by simply going to a Mercedes dealership, buying cars and paying with checks. Then I turn around and sell them to a nice guy at the street corner for half the price, getting paid with checks drawn on some Russian bank. I don't know why, but he is totally eager to buy everything I can supply to him on those terms.

You can immediately see how I am losing huge amounts of money because I am giving away cars for at best half their real value. But it must be good, it produces large numbers for the revenue, right?

Of course not. Revenue is a number used for calculation. Revenue by itself doesn't tell you much – you have to combine it with the other numbers, such as costs of goods sold, marketing expenses, and cash flows.

A statement like "I made half a million" says absolutely nothing. And probably that is precisely its purpose.

Entities:
Welcome to the Danger Zone

No matter whether you were talking with business advisers, attorneys or accountants – sooner or later the topic of entities will have come up. Chances are, your eyes glazed over and you mumbled something like "huh?" or another comment of similar sophistication.

Lacking any remote idea of what those guys are talking about, your business choices most likely defaulted to "the least-effort version" – so you ended up with something called a "sole proprietorship" (that's what most self-employed usually default to).

What is an entity – and why would you care?

The term "entity" simply is a catch-all term for all imaginable combinations of legal structure and taxation choices for your operations.

Can't you simply call that a "business?"

Well... yes, you could. But what are you going to do about the myriads of non-profit organizations, facing similar decisions? Those you surely can't call businesses, right?

Why not call it partnerships?

For two reasons: first, the term "partnership" is already occupied by something very specific. And second, if you are just on your own – that wouldn't make it a partnership, would it?

Ok – why not just make up a term and use this made-up term for the whole bunch of these things?

Great suggestion! Let's invent the term "entity" and use it as a general term for all types of businesses and organizations!

There you have it – "entity" is simply the general term used when talking about a person or organization who needs to behave in some kind of business-like manner. That can be a single individual running some kind of business, it also may be a bunch of people operating or owning a business, but it also can be a non-profit organization of any size.

Using "entity" instead of the correct respective term makes it easier to write books about it, you know... it is just far more convenient to say

"an important aspect of **entity** selection is the matter of taxation"

rather than using the somewhat clunky

"an important aspect when selecting between **sole proprietorship, a limited or a general partnership, a corporation or a limited liability company, or even a limited liability partnership** is the matter of taxation."

The latter, less eloquent version additionally suffers the problem that it quickly gets outdated every time a state invents yet another legal structure to use. And it fails to include all the wonderful (and mostly useless) combinations of more than one legal structure to form a single business.

Yes, you can combine these things. And why in the world would you do that? I'm glad you asked – we will get back to that a bit later.

"Mostly useless" is not the same as "always useless"; in a few select cases, amalgamating entities to operate a single business actually does make sense, as you will see down the road; especially if and when you plan to do business in California (see the chapter "Entitetris" on page 41).

Liabilities, Taxes and Snags – oh my!

Would you prefer a meal called "Five ants crossing a bridge", or does "Buddha jumps over the wall" sound more enticing to you?

Unless you know what those two (obviously Chinese) dishes are, you couldn't tell with any degree of certainty, right?

But instead of having each of the recipes explained in painstaking detail, you may be able to narrow it down to "I am looking for something with pork today," or – if that suits you more – "I only eat vegetarian". Regardless of what the recipe says in details like sauces and spices, those simple aspects of your preferences rule out the biggest issues right away.

If you then can add "and by the way, I am allergic to celery and peanuts" – that puts you on the safer side of things. Still without really knowing anything about the intricacies of the recipe.

See, you don't have to know all details in order to make an informed and fairly safe choice. You just need to put out on the table what's important to you.

That said, what is it that's important to you when starting your business? Of course, I can't know that for sure. But let me propose three aspects of which I believe they **should** be important to you:

- Liability – what risks are you facing?
- Taxes – how much is the government taking? And why?
- Bureaucratic complexity – how much of your time and sanity will it take to comply with the legal requirements?

Let's briefly run through those, and you will get an idea of why I think they are important.

Liability – what does it mean?

Whenever you cause any harm or damages to somebody else, you are responsible to pay for the repair of that damage. Plus whatever side costs it may have caused.

If, for instance, you did push somebody in front of a car, you are obviously required to pay the medical bills and the car repair. But that's not all – the person suffering from your action wasn't able to earn income while being in a hospital and maybe long time thereafter; so, you are also responsible to pay up for this lost income. The same holds true for the owner of the car: while the garage guys are repairing the car, the vehicle is not available for the owner to use. Therefore, the owner will have to rent another car, for example – and those costs you also will have to bite.

Last, but not least, there is the suffering itself, the pain you inflicted on others. For that, the court will make you pay as well. In recent years it has become clear that this component easily can be the largest of the costs involved.

This financial responsibility for your actions is called liability.

There is another type of responsibility – the criminal aspect of it. Regardless of any civil liability, the rule of thumb is: if it can be shown that you did "it" intentionally, then you are on the hook for criminal behavior.

You may have purchased liability insurance, which covers the financial demands the court places on you for what you did. But the insurance company certainly will not go to prison on your behalf – that still remains your personal "job".

So, you can incur criminal liabilities and civil liabilities (the latter mostly meaning that you have to pay for some damages you caused).

We're living in a society with so many rules and laws that it is almost impossible to **not** break at least one of those – and while it is unlikely that you won't notice when you're breaking Baltimore's ban on igniting thermonuclear bombs within city limits, there are many less obvious cases of violating some kind of rule or ordinance.

Let's have a look at a common situation your business might find itself in: a customer handed a device to you in order to check it for problems. Now it might just happen that you inadvertently push it off the table. The device falls down to the floor and breaks. Happens, right?

Well – you just violated your fiduciary duty. If you are handed something which isn't yours, you are required to handle it with utmost care and make sure you can return it undamaged to the proper owner. If you are damaging it instead, you have incurred a liability: while the owner probably will not press criminal charges (if it's obviously an accident), she still will want to get reimbursed for the costs of buying a new one. And there you have your liability – unintended, unplanned, but still costing you money.

Another type of liability can be easily and unknowingly incurred whenever you use anything which is **not** created by yourself. You have a website and are using a nice picture you found on the internet? Gosh, you may just have infringed on somebody's copyright – and that person will come after you and demand payment, sooner or later.

And no, talking your way out of something doesn't work. I myself have been the owner of a trademarked name – and when I approached another business (which some years later thought they really liked that name) and asked them to stop using it, they seriously told me "We tried to reach you by email and get your permission. But since you didn't respond, that was good enough and now we can use it."

Well – no, it doesn't work that way. If somebody holds a copyright, trademark or patent, then you need that somebody's permission to use it. If you are using such a thing without permission, you have made yourself liable to (substantial) financial liabilities. The owner of the trademark can demand (and enforce) compensation for that usage back to the first day you did use it. Regardless of whether you knew you were infringing or not!

Let's assume you didn't know – and you have been infringing on somebody's trademarks or copyrights for some years before they found out. The compensation payment, depending on how much else was involved in your sales, can easily eat up your entire sales revenue of those years. On top of that, you will have to pay for legal fees. In other words: those incidents can easily break you and take everything you have. And then some. A simple picture on a website or on your product can do that to you.

Even if you bought the picture – how did you make sure the person "selling" it to you did have the right to do so? At some time, you will just have to stop researching it and hope for the best... and incur a huge liability risk.

Now look at your business: Let's say you have sales revenue of $200,000 from the infringing product. All-in, you may end up having to pay $300,000 for that copyright liability issue. Does your business have those 300K at hand, so you can pay it off right away? Well, with only 200K of revenue, chances are: you don't have enough money, even if you have a high profit margin.

What's happening next? Can the copyright owner's attorney come after everything your company owns? Yes!

Can that attorney come after anything and everything you and your family own? Now **that** depends – this is the difference between unlimited liability and limited liability. In case of unlimited liability, the buck stops with the business entity: they can take everything which this business owns, they can even take the business itself. But they cannot take from your personal assets.

If you are operating an entity with unlimited liability, then yes: as the term "unlimited" implies, you will be held liable with no limits. Everything you own and will own (and, to a degree, have previously owned) is at risk of being seized and handed to the victim of your infringement. Keep in mind:

Legally, the copyright owner is the victim – not you! You are just suffering the consequences of being careless.

I know, when you are in this position, it certainly feels the other way around. Been there, done that, got that t-shirt. The almost inevitable outcome is personal bankruptcy.

Sorry, did I just scare you?

Good!

I guess we can agree that it's at least worth having a look at how well each of the entity types can protect your private assets. But again, please note: whatever is in the name of your business, is always on the hook for business liabilities, no matter the type of entity!

Taxes

When we hear "taxes", we first think "1040". That's the annual return for the Federal individual income tax, as demanded by the IRS. Most states have their own version of it, too.

But the income tax for many people is not even the biggest chunk of the tax bite. Have a look at your pay stub (or last year's W-2) – you should be able to find two positions called "Social Security Tax" and "Medicare Tax". Those two combined make up about 7.65% of your wages – and are taken out right away.

Those 7.65% are literally only half the truth. Your employer pays the same amount on top of your share. Now, you might wonder what the employer's share has to do with you. Think again: where do you think the so-called employer's share does come from?

Obviously, the employer has to earn it somehow. **Somehow?**

Yeah... this "somehow" simply means: whatever your labor is worth, the employer has to first take out half of those Social Security and Medicare Taxes. Only what is left over, the employer then can pay you as wages or salary – and from that amount, you are paying your half of those taxes. In other words: your labor has to pay for both halves anyway. Whether or not you see it, the real tax rate for the two combined runs at 15.3% - or in other words, almost one-sixth of your salary.

If you are self-employed, you will have to pay both halves of it – then it's called "Self-Employment Tax" (SE-Tax); but it's really identical with the amount employees pay – the politicians just didn't find a way to hide half of the amount from the tax returns of self-employer taxpayers.

Sooo – you are really paying two different taxes to the Federal government, before even moving on to the state level. One tax is the income tax, which is calculated based on your total income for the year. The higher your income, the more of each additional dollar will be taken out as taxes.

The other tax is the FICA tax (=Social Security + Medicare), which is a constant 15.3%, at least for the first roughly $130.000 (thereafter, only Medicare Tax applies to additional dollars; Social Security Tax has a maximum amount of roughly $8000 per person and year).

Why is that important? Well – FICA tax does neither care about your personal deductions nor about your adjustments to income (such as student loan interests, IRA and 401k contributions, or anything like that). If, for example, you are earning a $50.000 salary per year, your FICA tax is higher than your income tax. Due to their little gimmicks, it doesn't look like this on your W-2, much less on the tax return – but that's actually the way the cookie crumbles.

Not even income tax credits will allow you to reduce your FICA burden, simply because they are credits against the **income tax**. If there is no income tax, those credits are usually falling off the wagon – what stays on, though, happens to be the FICA tax.

Employees don't spend much thought on their Social Security and Medicare taxes; the amounts are taken out of the paychecks, and that's about it.

Self-employed people, however, have to pony up the amounts based on their profits – which most likely are heavily fluctuating. Unless you're having your **ongoing** accounting done by an accountant, chances are you will be caught at tax time like a deer in the headlight. Those 15.3% very often come quite unexpected for starting self-employeds. And that's a pity.

If you made $100K, spent most of that as a down payment for your new home and living expenses – and then are expected to pay $15300 SE-tax plus, let's say, $20K for income taxes... ouch. You didn't see this $35.300 tax burden coming, did you?

It may come as a surprise to learn that SE-tax is not the same across the board. Here, too, it depends on the entity type how much of the business' earnings are subject to this SE-tax – and if any **at all**.

Look out for the FICA/SE tax treatment of the business income – it depends on the chosen entity; therefore, you should take that into consideration when choosing.

Snags – how complex is the paperwork?

On one hand, most business starters seem to believe that all businesses cause the same amount of paperwork headache. On the other hand, when asked why they are using a sole proprietorship as entity type, the common response is "it was the easiest".

Well... apparently there **is** a difference between entities – and intuitively we are aware of that. Just – how much of a difference? Does it matter?

As you undoubtedly have figured out by now: if it wouldn't matter, I would not bother to talk about it here. So – yes, paperwork **does matter**. In surprisingly many cases, the mere fact of having to do all that paperwork, fill out forms and stuff like that – just the fact of having to do that **can** and **often does** trigger depressions. I am serious! Not just metaphorically speaking, no... I am talking real clinical depressions. Nothing kills your business and your family faster than depressions. So, as a rule of thumb: try to get by with as little **required** legal paperwork as you can – the proper choice of entity goes a long way to help you with this goal.

That of course doesn't mean you should skip the papers you are required to do. Rather, I am suggesting to make your upfront decisions in a way which doesn't end up swamping you in formal requirements later on.

Take a sole proprietorship as example: there is no paperwork required for this entity type at all. Your business is identical to yourself, and you cannot even enter into contracts with yourself – great, so no unnecessary forms.

On the other side of the spectrum, there is the corporation. Just setting it up requires a whole lot of paper; shutting it down is even worse. But those two don't matter much if you want to run the business for a long time. So, everything is good? Far from it. Corporations are required to have a board, an executive officer and a chairman. Not to forget the shareholders and their annual meeting. Yes, in most states that all can be the same person. **But** you are still required to have regular board meetings (you, you and you), for which all discussions and decisions have to be written down and archived. Any change in your salary needs to have similar meeting formalities attached to it.

Oh, you forgot something in the corporate minutes which is needed afterwards for a lawsuit? Too bad – if it's not in there, it didn't happen.

If you don't follow all corporate rules to the last dot, any attacking attorney will tear your corporation apart – holding your personally liable for all issues which can be even remotely traced to your negligence (which in practice means: pretty much everything).

So – while in theory corporations provide you with liability protection, the **real** fact is: your entity protects you only until you fail to follow through on the legal requirements for that very entity. Corporations are notoriously bad for small businesses – unless juggling paperwork is a favorite pastime of yours.

Even worse: if you don't follow corporate laws and its bylaws diligently, not only will your liability protection fall apart – your negligence by itself will trigger a whole new set of dangers for additional liabilities which doesn't even exist for other types of entities. Even when you are the sole shareholder of that corporation, your own corporation can still be forced to bring lawsuit against you for breach of fiduciary duties.

In other words: if you opt for a corporation as entity of choice, you better have an attorney at hand who checks your meeting paperwork while things are going on. No, you cannot "do it later" – that's illegal, to begin with. And there will be no time to fix the issues once you have a sheriff in the doorframe who wants to seize your corporate records for a law case.

Let me be clear: these legal requirements **are the same** for S-Corporations as they are for C-Corporations. The difference between "S" and "C" is only for taxation purposes – it has nothing to do with commercial laws and corporate records. I am pointing that out because I have heard far too often statements like "Don't worry, that stuff doesn't apply to me – I have elected to be an S-Corporation." No, you didn't – because you can't. You may have elected to **be taxed** as an S-Corporation. But this election is just between the IRS and your corporation – no plaintiff attorney cares about your choices of taxation, nor does he have to. Sorry to be bearer of bad news…

Now what?

Those three main points frame the ground you need to cover when making your entity choice. But – which are the options you have? And which one is the right one?

I am so glad you decided to ask! That's what the next sections are intended to guide you through.

What's a sole proprietorship?

The simplest entity one can imagine is the so-called **sole proprietorship**, and many sole proprietors don't even know that's what they are. They usually call themselves "freelancers" or "self-employed" – but if they are on their own and have made no other choice of entity, they are operating as sole proprietors.

Liability protection

That's easy: there is none.

Whatever the business is liable for, you will be held liable for as well. For an outsider, you **are** your business.

Taxes

Your business does its accounting stuff, and the result goes on Schedule C **and** on Schedule SE of your individual tax return (IRS form 1040); for the state you are living in, the handling is mostly the same – just the form numbers vary.

What that means is: on the first $128K, you are taxed with income tax **and** 15.3% SE-Tax. On everything above that threshold, you are taxed with income tax **and** 2.9% Medicare tax (Social Security Tax is capped, Medicare Tax is not).

Oftentimes, business owners have heard something about "double taxation" of corporations – but sole proprietors have their own version of double taxation as well: On half of the SE-tax, you also must pay income tax. Yeah, you read that right: even though the government is taking that SE-tax from you, they are still taxing you on half of it as if it were income to you.

So – as a sole proprietor (living single) you pay at least 15.3% tax even on the first $1000 you make in a year. While the first $12000 are free of income tax (thanks to the standard deduction), no white knight comes to the rescue from SE-tax. So, even for the "tax-free" base amount of $12000 per year, you are going to pay about $1800 taxes.

Bureaucratic complexity

The sole proprietorship doesn't establish any liability limitation whatsoever, and it isn't taxed as anything on its own – so it must be the entity type with the least paperwork involved.

While in theory that is actually true, a sole proprietorship comes with its own set of bureaucratic worms – namely the problem that the business is impossible to distinguish from the individual person that you are. This problem makes you lose some taxation benefits of businesses that you otherwise could enjoy. But probably worse: your business is going to mess up your personal credit file.

Why would there be a problem with your credit file?

Well, **personal** credit files are expected to reflect **personal** affairs. Private individuals usually don't have annual salaries of several million dollars.

Now imagine you own and operate a retail company. In this case, your turnover might well end up in the multi-million-dollar range. But please, don't confuse turnover with income or profit. Turnover is just what's keeping your boxes moving – you cannot use that money to spend on any private desires.

How are you going to handle those numbers, when your credit cards (based on your social security number) are giving you a mere 10K credit limit?

Assumed you can convince a credit card lender to increase the limit appropriately to, let's say, $100K.

Then you want to purchase a home and apply for a mortgage loan. The lender almost surely will request your personal tax returns of recent years. What will he see? Well, probably a tax return showing something like $40K income per year. And a credit file showing a $100K credit card, of which probably half is used up right now.

Oops – you are owing more on a credit card than you make in an entire year? Your home **loan application is declined**.

And they probably won't even tell you the reason for the decision.

That's because personal credit is something entirely different than business credit – we will look into this later in this book, and I promise you: there are surprises waiting for you.

As a sole proprietor, you have virtually no chance of building up your business credit. But you can easily destroy your personal credit standing.

Partnership – General or Limited?

Partnerships are what you get when a bunch of people do something together without setting up an entity structure. So, whenever you think you are just renting an office together or you are selling some stuff together, but "everybody does his own thing" – you are most likely wrong. That's how you form a "general partnership". You can register a general partnership in most states – but you don't have to.

A special case of a partnership is the "Limited Partnership", often abbreviated as "LP". The word "limited" refers to the fact that at least one partner enjoys limited liability.

The Limited Partnership needs to be registered because otherwise nobody would know about it being "limited" in any way.

Limited partnerships have two classes of partners. While every partnership has at least one "General Partner", Limited Partnerships additionally have at least one Limited Partner.

General Partners

A general partner is more or less self-employed like in a sole proprietorship. Except – he's not "sole".

You can think of this as the worst of all worlds: you don't get to keep all the profits because you have to share. But every general partner can screw up all by himself and still cause damage to all partners.

General partners are running the business, they represent it and they all have full power for decisions – every general partner individually. Even if your contract says otherwise, outsiders are not required to recognize your internal rules. That means: if one partner screws up and oversteps his boundaries, that's a problem between you partners internally – any creditor or plaintiff can approach you on behalf of the partnership and hold you liable, no matter who really caused a problem.

Limited Partners

This type of partner occurs only in limited partnerships. A limited partner is prohibited from "materially participating in business decisions". Whatever that means in any particular case. Essentially, for the limited partner, that means: stay out of the business.

Traditionally, limited partners contribute cash (or other forms of capital) to the business, while the general partner does the work.

Liability Protection in Partnerships

There is no protection for the general partners. Each of them is fully liable for all liabilities of the partnership – and I want to point it out again: that includes those liabilities another general partner has caused. So, if another general partner hits a person with a car while claiming to be on a business tour, all general partners (including you) are on the hook for any damages from that accident. If the damaged person can get the most money from you, she or he can do so – there is no "fair share of the costs" or anything like that. Instead: every general partner is fully liable. For everything.

Did I mention that I think a partnership with more than one general partner is a bad idea?

The limited partner, on the other hand, enjoys protection. Limited partners can only lose their contribution to the business (some adjustments are made if the partner got money from the business before that money was really earned – those monies the limited partner may have to pay back to the company in case of a liability law suit).

Taxes for Partnerships

For federal tax purposes, partnerships don't have to pay taxes. Instead, their income is apportioned to the partners – and it ends up on the individual partners' tax returns (usually a 1040).

General partners are very much like sole proprietors, but instead of your personal 1040 Schedule C, the income will go to Schedule E of the very same form 1040. And, of course, to Schedule SE. Yes, that means: general partners in a partnership are paying 15.3% SE-tax on their share of the business income.

For limited partners, things looks a bit better: since they didn't materially participate in the business, their share of the income is not considered "self-employment income". Therefore, no SE-tax applies.

Instead, the limited partner's share of the taxable income goes on form 1040 **only** to Schedule E – that means: income will be taxed at the partner's individual tax bracket rate, while losses from the partnership will reduce the overall taxable income (and thereby usually save some taxes).

For Federal taxes, partnerships must file form 1065 – on the Schedule K-1 (1065), each partner gets assigned his or her share of the business income or loss. Obviously, the numbers for all partners combined must be the same as for the business as a whole. After all, the IRS wants to collect taxes on all of the income, right?

For the individual states, a similar partnership return is filed – for pretty much the same purpose.

Some states (California for example) are imposing an additional annual fee on **limited** partnerships.

Bureaucratic complexity

General partnerships come into existence faster than you may think, and often inadvertently so. That also means: for general partnerships, there is little legal paperwork required (actually none; but I strongly suggest you write some – just so you have a mutual understanding of the rights and duties each partner has).

While the law doesn't require limited partnerships to have a written agreement, it is almost inevitable to have one nevertheless – how else would anybody be able to prove how much of a partnership's loss the limited partners have to bear?

I can almost hear it "We have a loss of more than $12K – you agreed to pay for that $10.000 of that loss." – "No, I didn't. I said I would pay $1.000…"

Sometimes, a written agreement helps save lives. As you can see.

Corporation

Typically abbreviated as Corp or Inc, the corporation is probably the oldest entity type for which legal paperwork is required. That's intentional – the first corporation was set up by the English King and his buddies, in order to limited their liability from operating merchant ships.

That gives you a good clue at whom the corporate legal structure is targeted: people with lots of money and good government connections.

Admittedly, that's not who uses corporations these days, and certainly not in the US. Nevertheless, the legal requirements still very much show their origins.

Keep that in mind when hearing about all those gosh wonderful corporate paradises like Delaware. Indeed, they **are** corporate paradises. For example, Delaware gives the corporate management a lot of power against its shareholders, so the corporate board oftentimes can void or at least delay shareholders' decisions.

Now let me ask you: do you want your corporate management to block you as an owner? Hardly. When you are setting up a new company, you want the ability to steer and control your business – and what Delaware hands to the management is the exact opposite of what you want.

So – if you are the CEO of somebody else's corporation, Delaware may seem like a good place to move your legal incorporation to, especially if you are intending to take the control out of the owner's hands. If you are an owner or the founder, such considerations should have no place in your life!

Liability protection

Traditionally, the corporation's protection for the shareholders is excellent. Protection for the management – less so. Yes, the corporate laws provide extensive protection to the managers as well, **if and only if** every "t" is crossed and every "i" is dotted.

Corporations are, almost by definition, bureaucratic beyond your wildest fears – and while you have idle sunshine, everything seems fine even if you didn't take the paperwork obligations too serious. Things change dramatically when the wind picks up and the sea gets rougher. One of the first things an attacking attorney will request from you are the corporate minutes of recent years and of course the bylaws, as well as your board's decisions regarding your compensation and so on.

Any of that missing or not saying exactly the same thing that you have been doing in reality afterwards? That's an "oops" moment – you're toast.

If just one aspect is even remotely fishy – forget any liability protection. The courts are kind of merciless when it comes to assumed abuse of the corporate structure (which is precisely what you have done in their opinion).

Even if something went wrong **without you being at fault** – if you are the CEO and therefore in charge of the records: if anything is missing or wrong with the records, you'll be on the hook. With everything you own and will own.

Taxes for Corporations

Surprisingly, the tax laws for corporations have been modernized much faster than the commercial laws. As a result, corporations have mainly two different choices of how they want to be taxed. Plus some decisions by the IRS, which I would hardly consider a "choice", at least not in the good meaning.

The traditional (and standard) taxation system for a corporation is the so-called "C" corporation; the appropriate tax form to be filed annually is form 1120.

C-Corp (taxed according to subchapter "C")

When taxed as a "C-Corp", the corporation determines its corporate income and pays a flat 21% tax on that income – no matter how high it is. Please note: after paying the tax, the remaining profits are still inside the corporation. If you want to take them out and use them for personal spending, you will have to pay a dividend to the shareholder (you) – for which you personally will be taxed on your income tax return! (That's where the infamous buzzword "double taxation" comes from – the income is taxed at the corporate level, and after you take it out of the corporation, it's taxed again at the personal level.) However, dividends are **not** subject to SE-tax.

To avoid abuse of the favorable 21% tax rate (which is way lower than the tax rate on high-income individuals), there are two special cases which are essentially punishments:

If most of the corporation's revenue is derived from work you personally are doing (if you are an accountant, an attorney, a model, a singer...), then your corporation will be qualified as a "Personal Service Corporation" (PSC) – and you will pay a high penalty tax.

Something similar happens when you are keeping many passive-income or portfolio-income sources inside your corporation, for example real estate or stocks and bonds. Then you will be qualified as a "Personal Holding Corporation" (PHC) – and again, you will pay a high penalty tax. Real-estate professionals, though, are rescued from this penalty: if more than 60% of the corporation's income comes from real estate **and** you can show that more than half of the rest **is not** portfolio income, then you qualify as a real estate corporation and will be spared the penalty. **If you are doing real estate, ask your attorney and your accountant!**

S-Corp (taxed according to subchapter "S")

Most people memorize the S-corporation as "small corporation". That's not what it meant, but it's a good way to mentally sort those abbreviations.

The s-corporation was introduced to accommodate the small business way of doing things. The main difference to a c-corp is the fact that an s-corp is a flow-through entity. That means: the income (or loss) from the s-corporation flows through to the owners' individual tax return. The corporate income is **not** taxed at the corporate level.

Although the s-corp does file an own tax return (form 1120-S), this is just an information return and doesn't trigger corporate income tax.

The corporate income of an s-corp is treated almost like the income share for limited partners in a partnership. Whichever income share comes out of the s-corporation goes directly to the shareholders' Schedule E of form 1040 – and therefore will be included in the 1040 tax return.

That's especially beneficial if you are expecting initial losses in your corporation: in that case, the loss flows through to your 1040 and lowers your income. If you have other income (from salary, for example), you may end up with a nice tax refund come April 15.

Income flowing through from an s-corp is **not** subject to SE-tax because it is considered a dividend.

However, you **are** required to pay yourself a salary, if you are participating in the corporation (which most likely you are, since you probably will be the managing owner, which is called chief executive officer). This salary **will** be subject to the normal FICA tax (Social Security and Medicare Tax, to refresh your memory) totaling 15.3% of your gross salary.

How much salary should your corporation pay you?

Ask your CPA; they have lookup tables for your industry – and the guidelines from the tables, applied to your profits, will give your CPA a good idea how much (or little) of salary you can get away with.

The part you pay **as salary** to yourself obviously doesn't get included in your dividend share – so in effect the real question difference between your two types of income from that one s-corp only is: will the income be subject to SE-tax (or FICA-tax), or will it not?

Now, S or C ?

If you are running the risk of being qualified as a personal service corporation or a personal holding corporation – you don't have much of a choice: you will go with the "S" election and be taxed as an s-corp (simply because there is no penalty tax for the s-corp, while for the c-corp there is).

If you are expecting initial losses, at least for tax purposes, you probably will also elect the s-corp. That allows you to take the losses on your 1040 and claw back some of your hard-earned taxes which have been taken out of your paycheck from other companies (or from your own corporation!).

If you have employees or contractors doing the main work in your business **and** you expect the business to produce profits from year #1, you might want to consider "C" status for your corporation. That would give you the nice 21% tax rate for the amount you keep in the corporation for future growth.

Fortunately, you don't even have to use a crystal ball – you can change this election as you go, and you can make it after you know the result for your first year. How cool is that? **Ask your CPA!**

But please note:

S-corp and c-corp are elections you are making for your **existing** corporation, and it is an election for tax purposes only. You cannot "incorporate an s-corporation".

There is no such thing as an s-corp for legal purposes. Both taxation types are still dealing with legally the same thing: a corporation.

Bureaucratic complexity

The complexity and error-proneness of corporations is legendary. A single paper missing or forgotten to be signed – and you have opened a whole can of worms. Those worms are likely to never get back into the can, either.

While all other entity structures run into their respective issues right away, and usually those issues have to do with the owners/partners or the government (be it the secretary of state or the IRS) – all of which can be fixed fairly easy – **the corporation is different**.

Technically, a corporation is as easy to set up as any other structure. The problems come when you get sued by someone: at that time, you will notice there have been a gazillion of rules and laws you should have been following all along but didn't.

As a result, is has become a sort of habit for courts to basically assume they can throw out the liability protection by default – and only grant it back if you can prove everything is exactly as required. Knowing small business owners, I venture out to say: you probably will not be able to prove it and in consequence, you will suffer.

Therefore: Unless you take extraordinary precautions, your corporation will not protect you from anything. At least not if an attacking attorney knows what he's doing.

Why am I discussing this so intensely if the corporation is no good anyway?

Not so fast – continue to read on, there's help to the rescue.

Limited Liability Company (usually abbreviated as LLC or LC)

First of all: don't call this thing a "corporation". An LLC is **not** a corporation at all, and you don't "incorporate" an LLC, either. For which, by the way, you should be very grateful.

You are "forming" or "organizing" an LLC, and it is a limited liability **company**, not *corporation*. Getting those terms mixed up is an open invitation for fraudsters and banksters to take advantage of you – because you clearly have no clue of what you are doing! If you call your LLC a "corporation", they have to assume you made other mistakes in your papers as well. Ok, now I can get off that soap box... and don't feel bad if you mix it up: politicians do it all the time, too.

The LLC and the LLP are currently the youngest general-purpose business entity structures. They have been created by the states in an attempt to fix major shortcomings of the other entity with limited liability (the corporation).

And boy, did they fix it. The states' work on the LLCs was nothing short of spectacular. In combination with frustration on the side of Congress, the IRS essentially threw their hands up in the air and said "We're not going to invent **yet another** way to tax a business."

The LLC has gone from "Stay away from it, nobody really knows how to deal with it" all the way to "Because there is no predefined way how it is dealt with, you as the owner have the choices and all the power!"

That's what I call a long journey.

Since LLCs have mostly just one type of member, the LLC must have some paperwork stating who the manager of the LLC is supposed to be (and how one can be elected or removed) – commonly, this ends up written into the Operating Agreement.

LLCs can be formed with one or more members (in contrast, partnerships always require at least two partners).

Liability protection

As the name implies, LLCs grant liability limitation to the owners (called "LLC members").

Similar to the limited partners with a limited partnership, all members enjoy this limited liability treatment – and in case of an LLC, that even includes the member who is running the business. Please recall: limited partners of a partnership can **not** materially participate in the business. In case of an LLC, it doesn't matter whether or not they participate.

The manager (or the managing member) has to make sure his distributions to members don't hurt the business; that aside, you have pretty good protection against the oddities of business life.

Taxes

I mentioned above, Congress and the IRS have given up on creating new tax laws for the LLC. So – how is it taxed?

Well... that's up to you. Really.

The LLC can choose to be taxed as a corporation or as a partnership. Or, if only 1 member exists, as a sole proprietorship – which is called "disregarded entity" because in this case the LLC is taxed as if it didn't exist, just as a sole proprietor is not separate from his business.

You may recall – corporations themselves also have a choice: either c-corp or s-corp. And since LLCs can choose to be taxed as corporations, LLCs have this choice available to them, too!

Therefore, an LLC can choose to be:

- taxed as a disregarded entity (i.e. sole proprietorship) if it has only 1 member
- taxed as a partnership if it has two or more members

- taxed as an s-corporation
- taxed as a c-corporation

That was easy – nothing new to learn.

If you have elected the c-corp status and you find out an s-corp status would have been better? Then your fictitious "tax-c-corporation" simply elects to now be taxed as an s-corp.

If you find out a partnership treatment would suit your LLC better? Then the LLC will elect to be treated as a partnership for tax purposes.

It really is that easy. You can flip between the taxation systems without having to set up a new entity. You will keep all the same, and nobody on the outside will know. Why should they? Even the LLC's EIN stays the same.

That has serious advantages for your business credit and your contracts, as we will see later in this book.

Of course, there are certainly tax regulations to prevent abuse of this flexibility – the IRS will make sure everything gets taxed at least once. Therefore – **ask your accountant!**

At the state level, most states follow the federal tax election. However, you will frequently find an additional tax imposed on LLCs, sometimes depending on whether or not the LLC opted to be treated as a corporation (often, those are the very same states which impose such taxes on corporations and limited partnerships as well – so essentially, they make sure they will get that tax from the LLC, no matter what. Yes, California, I am looking right at ya).

Bureaucratic complexity

From a paperwork point of view, LLCs are quite similar to Limited Partnerships – they don't need much in terms of papers, but they **should** have some.

Depending on your home state, you normally need to file some kind of document stating the creation of the LLC (often called "Articles of Organization") and a report that says who is authorized to speak and act for the LLC. In case of a corporation, those people would be called "officers", but in case of an LLC, most states allow you to call them whatever you want to call them. I have seen a company dealing in Christmas ornaments, where the company's manager was called "Archangel". So, yes, you can do that. The real question is: should you? Picture yourself negotiating a large loan for a real estate purchase – and when asked for your title, you have to respond "Archangel..."

Louisiana for example has two different paper forms for those two purposes (Articles of Organization, and Initial Report). Other states have just one form to put the information on.

In addition to the required paperwork, every LLC should have an "Operating Agreement". That paper should spell out how the manager is supposed to run the business – and what exactly that business is supposed to do. If you are more than just one member in your LLC, you will need the operating agreement for the same reason a limited partnership needs a document stating how profit and loss are split between the partners.

Even if you are a one-man show, it helps to write down intermediary goals as part of the operating agreement – because: if you choose the LLC to be taxed as a corporation, you can attach nice tax-free bonuses to reaching those goals. And who doesn't like the sound of "tax-free"?

Also, if your business performance falls short of your own expectations, that might just be a reason to cut your salary (when taxed as a corporation) – which also conveniently cuts the FICA tax burden. Always good if the IRS has the documents way before that cut happens – this way, they can't claim it's a decision only related to taxes.

Limited Liability Partnership (usually abbreviated as LLP)

The LLP is targeted at professionals (accountants, attorneys, and such). The main difference to an LLC is: in case of an LLC, a manager has to be appointed. Failing to do so means: nobody can run the LLC.

In case of an LLP, it starts from the opposite extreme: all members are allowed to run the partnership. The partnership agreement would have to exclude specific individuals from running the business (awkward...)

Liability protection

Essentially the same as for an LLC. It is important to keep in mind: since LLPs have more than one persons in charge of decisions, that usually also means: the business is at risk stemming from decisions of multiple persons at the same time - independently. In other words: every member can ruin the LLP.

Taxes

Essentially the same as for LLCs; however, since LLPs are intended for use by professionals, the election to be taxed as a c-corporation should be ruled out entirely.

The reason: professional services would turn any c-corporation into a PSC (personal service corporation), which is tax-penalized. The same applies to an LLP taxed as a c-corp. So, don't do that.

Bureaucratic complexity

Essentially identical to an LLC or a Limited Partnership.

Entitetris

Just to have mentioned it: each of the entities discussed has some kind of legal personality. Therefore, it can do whatever any other person could do. That includes being part of another entity.

Traditionally you would come up with some combination structure if you want to do something clearly not intended. Before the LLC was invented, an outcome similar to an LLC often was composed by using a corporation as the general partner of a limited partnership. That gives the limited partners their usual role as sources of capital with little say in the business, while the general partner endures unlimited liability. Since that general partner happened to be a corporation, the danger of unlimited risk is kind of moot – yes, the corporation is unlimited liable for the LP. The owner of the corporation, however, is not liable for the business, but nevertheless in control of the corporation and therefore of the entire LP.

As said, nowadays we use LLCs for those purposes – the combined structure of corp & LP is kind of outdated.

However, there are still situations for which combinations actually make sense.

Assume for a moment you are doing business mainly in California (as bad as this idea may be). That requires you to register with California. Further, you do business in Louisiana and Utah, Nevada and Texas.

All of those states require you to register there. And especially California slaps you with a sizeable fee for just being a corporation, an LLC or even an LP. No such fee if you form a general partnership – but who would want a general partnership with unlimited liability, really?

Here's an idea for your attorney and your accountant:

How about registering **two** LLCs in "easier" states like Louisiana or Utah? Instead of your LLC registering with California, a new entity does this registration: a **general partnership** with those other two LLCs as partners.

As California clearly states: merely being partner in a California partnership does **not** establish doing business in California. So, as far as California is concerned, you will be doing business there as a general partnership. Its liability, however, ends with the two LLCs. From your point of view:

same result. Except – no annual California fee for the LLC or a corporation. Cute, isn't it?

You do the same with the other states – and instead of having to pay several annual fees for LLC or corporations, you get away with the very low amounts for general partnerships. Those savings easily compensate for the overhead of one additional LLC in a low-cost state.

Just a little bit of thinking outside the box.

Choices, choices...

Now that we have all those options – what are we going to do with them? How in the world can you find the right one for you?

It's actually easier than you may think. For this discussion, I will assume:

- you are just one person wanting to go into business (that means, not a group of people)
- you are an US person for tax purposes (i.e. an American citizen or somebody with a permanent visa which grants residence and the right to self-employment)
- you want to run a business, rather than an investment scheme
- you plan to grow the business over time, rather than just going for a one-shot deal (a typical one-shot deal would have been selling sunglasses for the solar eclipse and then close the business down after the eclipse)

With all those options available, we can normally quickly rule out most of them:

- Sole Proprietorship: unlimited liability is no fun. If you cannot afford the $100 for forming another entity, you shouldn't be in business to begin with
- General Partnership: that's a sole proprietorship on steroids. Avoid it!

- Limited Partnership: If you are the one running the business, you will have no liability protection. Back to the sole proprietorship problem. So – no LP for you, either!
- Corporation: Seriously – if you are reading this book, then you probably shouldn't touch a corporation even with a pitch fork. Corporations are inherently complex beyond belief; failing on any single aspect will badly screw up your business and your life. Don't do it! Even the formerly main reason for incorporating (namely, listing a corporation at the stock exchange later in its life) is not valid anymore: by now, LLCs and even Limited Partnerships can be exchange-listed as well. And are, in large numbers.

What does that leave you with?

Given the title of my book, it should come as no surprise that the only things left over are the LLC and the LLP. Assuming you are not a licensed professional selling his time for money (accountant, attorney, …) – your only choice really is the LLC.

That's no problem – quite to the contrary. The LLC has the most up-to-date legal framework of all entities, and the IRS has found its own ways to use existing tax frameworks for it – green lights in all directions.

Where is the problem?

Accountants and Other Supernatural Beings

Taxation for LLCs is extremely flexible – you should hire an accountant to handle it, especially if you plan on taking advantage of flipping between different taxation methods.

The problem now is: accountants are usually good at accounting, and some are even brilliant when it comes to taxation. But they are hardly known for speaking plain English. Not only does their language include words which are **not** part of your everyday English – sometimes, they use a word almost in the opposite way a mortal human would.

That is a problem, and you will have to navigate through it. So, here is the biggest startup hurdle:

Many accountants tell you that an LLC is no good – you need to set up an S-Corp.

Is that the opposite of what I proposed? It sure sounds like it. Even a quite popular youtube presenter (accountant himself) repeats this statement over and over ad nauseam. Only after explicitly being asked what he thinks of an LLC *taxed as an S-Corp*, he revealed what he really tried to say all along:

"An LLC taxed as an S-Corp *is* an S-Corp for all intents and purposes. No, what I am saying: do not use an LLC *taxed as an LLC* because that's bad."

Erm... "taxed as an LLC"? In that moment, I wanted to yell out loud: there is no such thing as "being taxed as an LLC".

Of course, what he really was talking about was: an LLC taxed as a partnership.

And yes, I fully agree with him regarding this opinion. There are very few reasons to subject yourself to a partnership taxation if you have a choice to do otherwise.

But this accountant was so caught up in his daily accounting stuff that he called the standard taxation for LLCs (which is taxation as a partnership) *"taxed as an LLC"* – that little flaw may be unimportant for him. But it surely does confuse a lot of ordinary business people!

I know some cases where business starters have set up a corporation to operate the business – a real corporation, which is named that way and has only the "S" or "C" choices and nothing else. The sole reason for this potentially fateful decision was: the accountant said "LLCs are no good. Use a corporation."

The accountant was thinking of tax forms and taxation elections on those forms. The business owner didn't know that – and instead formed a legal structure which most likely will collapse under the first law suit because he didn't handle all legal requirements properly.

I have yet to find an accountant who insists on knowing all the ins and outs of legal paperwork for corporations, board meetings, shareholder meeting requirements and such. Yet, they are quick in telling you that you need a corporation.

So, keep in mind: when an accountant is talking to you – make sure to ask if she is referring to the actual legal entity "corporation", or whether he is just speaking of an entity *taxed as a corporation*. For an accountant – that's the same. For your attorney and you – not so much.

Taxation as a corporation or as partnership/sole prop?

With an LLC, you always have the option to choose sole proprietorship (if the LLC is owned by only one person), partnership (if owned by more than one person) or corporation as tax treatments.

As a rule of thumb, the taxation as corporation is the way to go for ongoing businesses. If you are already self-employed (or have self-employed income from a partnership) **and** your brand-new LLC produces startup tax losses – in **this case** it may be beneficial to choose the partnership/sole-prop taxation of your LLC.

If your LLC has been operating for a while and you want to shut it down for good, switching back to partnership/sole-prop taxation may be beneficial for the same reason: less hassles and some benefits on the SE-tax side. **Ask your CPA to calculate your specific case!** (Do not go for generalized catch-all statement "you never do this or that…" – there is almost always one case where that option is precisely what you need, and in those cases the benefit might end up being worth tens of thousands of dollars)

Taxed as C or S?

Once you have opted for taxation as a corporation – which is the most likely case – you also have to make the choice of going for the C or the S corporation.

Keep in mind – we are still talking about an LLC here. And more specifically, a small business with an LLC as its entity type. Small businesses have one thing in common: they are owned by small-business-owners. Small business owners, in turn, have one commonality as well: we are chronically bad at sticking to rules.

Legally, it is ok for you to take money out of the LLC and put it back into it two months later. Or the other way around.

For tax purposes, if you go for s-corporation status, you can get away with doing the money-in-and-out this way – you are taxed on your share of the profit, not on the amount you take out of the company.

For a c-corporation, however, things are quite different. Remember – a c-corporation pays its own taxes on the corporate profits. And whenever the shareholders receive a payment from the corporation, it's considered a dividend and therefore taxed again. See, in case of c-corporations, the mere movement of money from the company to your account (or wallet) indeed **does** trigger taxes. And no, you cannot make those taxes go away by putting the money back in.

So, some of the corporate complexities actually spill over into the taxation as a corporation.

Once you know that, you probably will want to go with the s-corporation, even if it is not necessarily the most tax-advantageous choice. But the mere chance of screwing things up are reason enough for many small business owners to avoid c-corp taxation like the plague.

But let's assume you do everything right and you have an accountant handling it properly and making sure you don't produce a total mess – what would be the other things you should take into consideration when making the selection between s-corp and c-corp?

Are you doing essentially all of the work?

If you are doing most the work in the business, you are at risk of being re-qualified as a PSC (personal service corporation). Selecting c-corp status as a PSC will slap you with a huge penalty tax – so, the only reasonable option left for you is the s-corp.

Is the company built on your personal reputation?

This case also will make it a PSC. The simple rule for personal service corporations: don't.

Choose s-corp status instead.

Will your business have a lot of portfolio or passive income?

Does your LLC hold any substantial sources of passive income? If so, it will be penalized for being a PHC, personal holding corporation. Same outcome as with PSCs – do not do that. Go for s-corp status in this case as well.

Passive income sources, by the way, are for example:

Real estate rentals (unless that's the only thing the company does), stock dividends, interests from investments and bank deposits, royalties from oil and gas wells, royalties for intellectual property of any kind (books, movies...) and such stuff. Essentially, passive income is everything you are always hoping for because it doesn't involve much work – and shouldn't be the dominant part in a c-corp. If you have it in your LLC, go for the s-corp election.

Does your LLC accumulate large amounts of unused money from previous profits?

If your LLC does accumulate large amounts of profits (larger than a quarter of a million) without paying it out to the owner(s) and you cannot immediately show the IRS the projected purpose of accumulating that money, as a c-corp you will be penalized with a special kind of tax. That's on top of the corporate income tax!

Yeah, you read that right – if your entity taxed as a c-corporation does accumulate too much money from profits, the IRS will take a part of it away. Ouch.

That doesn't apply if you can show that you are planning to buy a piece of real estate and you will need that money to pay for it. Or if you run a type of business where those accumulated amounts are fluctuating heavily, for example a movie production company or company which trades publishing rights – in those cases, you need large amounts of capital at your hands, so you can move quickly if an opportunity comes along.

But expect to be closely monitored – if you claim to need the cash at hand to buy publishing rights, but haven't done so five years in a row, then it's a sure-fire bet that the IRS will come back and impose the tax on you.

The reason for this tax is obvious: c-corporations are taxed at only 21%; it's tempting to simply keep the money in the company and have it grow while it's burdened with only the low corporate tax rate, instead of paying it out as dividends and subject it to the owner's tax rate again.

If the IRS figures out that's what you're doing, they will slap that accumulated earnings tax on you – and all benefits go out the window.

An s-corp, on the other hand, does have no such preferential 21% tax rate (s-corp earnings are taxed on your personal 1040) – so this additional tax trap doesn't apply to s-corps. Consequently, if you do accumulate such large earnings, you may want to opt for s-corp status.

Choice wrapped up in one sentence?

Unless yours is a special situation, you are likely to organize an LLC and opt for taxation as an s-corporation.

Because:

That will give you the full flexibility of an LLC, none of the legal headaches that come with a corporation, and a good handle on limiting the SE-tax to an amount absolutely necessary (instead of subjecting the entire earnings to the SE-tax, whether or not you received any of those earnings – that's what happens in partnerships).

The new 2018 flow-through discount

Completely new in the tax world for partnerships and s-corporations (included LLCs taxed as such) is the up to 20% discount on flow-through earnings from American businesses.

Up to 2017, whatever came out of a partnership or s-corp ending up on Schedule E of your 1040 was taxed at your normal tax rate.

Beginning 2018, that changed. To encourage small business startups and new hires of employees, now the flow-through earnings from partnerships and s-corps are discounted by up to 20% before being taxed on your 1040.

If you make $100K from your business, that way it could reduce your taxable income by $20K, which is a difference of approximately $4500 income tax. Having or not having $4500 occasionally does make a difference...

Alas, that's "up to 20%". There are additional limitations. If your business is a personal service business, you will get the full 20% discount, **but only** up to about $120K annual income. If you earn more, the discount is phased out.

If you are **not** a personal service business, then the permitted discount is calculated based on the payroll of your company and the business assets it owns (like machinery and office equipment) – frequently leaving you with much less than 20% as really permitted discount. But at least in turn you get the benefit of the discount not being phased out beyond a certain amount of income.

So, what's that supposed to do?

Making America great again, I guess. Let's think about it: all the professionals which cannot operate as a c-corp are now taxed as an s-corp. They will get the full 20% - but only if they don't make super-high income. If they do – no discount for them. If the idea was to give benefits to smaller accounting practices, but not the star attorneys: check, goal accomplished.

If you are **not** a professional and instead are running a "real" business, what are the largest expenses you will incur? Machines and payroll, commonly. Ok, those help with your discount.

What about the cases when you don't need machines or employees, but also are not a professional?

Then, it appears, you are not a desired business in the eyes of the tax reform act – you will fall short on the discount.

But hey, smile and be happy – at least they didn't throw a penalty tax at you (as they did with PSCs and PHCs when choosing c-corp status).

Business Credit

A common question you can find all over the internet – and (quite scaring) at business people's meetings – would have to be:

"How can I get funding for my business startup?"

The simple and most obvious answer to this question is: **you do not**. Except for: your own money.

That's not the response you wanted to hear, right? Yeah... thought so. But it's the truth.

Yes, I know quite well what you can hear and read elsewhere. From headlines promising $100,000 credit lines to million-dollar trade credit "in 90 days or less".

And admittedly, that might actually be true – because it is indeed possible. Just – it's not what you think it is.

Let me explain.

Equity and Credit – One of them can kill you

Sounds dramatic, but it's right on the mark. Equity is the term used for your own money. That's what the owners have provided to the company, and this money the company can use without having to pay it back.

The other type of capital is credit – that's what you can commonly get from banks and other lenders.

And then, there is stuff in between – depending on who's talking, it's called different names. For example, the capital contributed by limited partners is generally considered equity. But if you think about it: from **your** point of view (as the general partner), it's really just a long-term loan; the limited partners expect a certain return on their investment, and at some time you want to get them out of your business altogether. Yes, you will have to pay them off in this case – which is pretty much the same as repaying the loan.

The only difference between a limited partner and a lender is: the annual payment to the limited partner is usually not fixed but dependent on the business profits. And the limited partner commonly has some parts of the increased value of any business properties, be it real estate or royalty rights. So, the interest amount is the result of an annual calculation and does vary – but still, from your point of view, it's a situation quite similar to a loan: you have been provided with capital which you need to pay for and (at some time) repay.

The problem with credit – and especially with short-term credit such as the usual bank loans – is quite simple: that money needs to be repaid. Very soon.

You cannot afford to start the business, but you believe you can predict your ability to pay back a bank loan within a few months or years? Think again.

On top of that, a bank loan costs ongoing interests – usually monthly. In other words: it will be draining cash from your business at a time when you don't even have the money to start the business without that loan.

Can you spot the problem?

Cash Flow is King

For a moment, forget about all the tax stuff you are told. Yes, it's all important – but for now, put that on back burner.

Picture it: you are in the business of selling machines. You have a customer and need to deliver an XYZ-200 machine - which you do not currently have. How do you get this XYZ-200? Silly question – you buy it.

So, you buy it and pay... how?

Different question: in your opinion, how likely is that your phone company or your electricity company will wait until your business has generated enough money to pay them?

I can give you the answer: they won't.

Regardless of all taxation issues, regardless of anything else, there is **one thing** your business needs right from the get-go. That one thing is **cash flow** – which is simply the flow of incoming cash. And you need more cash coming in than going out (then it's called **positive cash flow**).

If you have no idea how to do that, then stop here – and rethink your entire business idea. You **must** have a clear plan how your business is supposed to generate enough cash flow to pay for the ongoing expenses.

If you take a loan from a bank, then you see the issue: the interests add to the ongoing expenses, making it even more difficult to come up with enough cash flow.

My first "real" company started with 100K in cash. You would think this should have been sufficient money to get a business off the ground, right?

Well – it wasn't. Not because there was not enough money. No, the real problem was that I really had no plan how to make it generate enough cash flow. Neither did my business partner, but we sure knew how to lease a car, a store front and add many other expenses.

Keep in mind: if you do not know how to create cash flow, you cannot replace that problem with more spending. It won't work. Not even if you call that spending "investing". I don't care how you call it. If it drains your cash flow, it's first and foremost **toxic**.

The cash flow of your business is its life blood. You can easily go broke showing large profits on your tax return. It's much rarer to go broke while large available cash flow is generated.

You want to tilt the odds in your favor: make cash flow and its protection your number one priority.

And that's where business credit comes into play.

The Function of Business Credit

Business credit (the ability to borrow) has exactly one purpose: protecting your cash flow and your cash in the bank.

You heard me. It is **not** purpose of credit to fund your everyday business expenses (nice word for "consumption"). It is **not** purpose of credit to pay for the inventory you purchased in the hope that it sells at some time. It is **not** purpose of credit to finance advertising campaigns, trade shows, lavish dinners or pay for First-Class airline tickets or hotels.

None of that.

You think it can do these things? Believe me: credit cannot do that. Credit needs to be paid back, and it gobbles up additional interests while waiting for the repayment. In effect, you have to pay more because you used credit. So – no, credit didn't pay for anything. Quite the opposite: credit does cost you money.

If you buy a whole bunch of stuff in good faith of finding customers quick enough before you have to pay the loan – then you may be a very faithful person, alas not a very responsible borrower. But soon a broke one.

All these things need to come out of your equity – that means: **your** money, or the money your company has made on past transactions.

How can credit protect your cash flow?

First of all, you need to be aware of what you can use credit for:

If your company has the cash sitting in an account, but you need to make several payments (say, getting fuel for your truck, which happens frequently in trucking businesses. At least one would hope so).

You surely don't want to keep all that money in the truck – or give an employed driver the cash to take with him. Instead – you pay the gas station with a charge card. At the time of the charge, you already have that money available – but by using the card, you are protecting your cash flow. The money won't get stolen, you have a paper trail for the IRS, and the more cash is sitting in the account, the more your bank will like you.

If you have a customer who already paid a substantial down payment on goods he ordered from you, then you can go ahead and use credit to buy those goods for delivery to the customer – you know you will get paid upon delivery (unless the customer is willing to lose the down payment). Again: the money to cover the deal is already waiting to do so; in this case, the same reasons apply for using credit. It protects your bank balance.

Really no case to be made for using credit to buy inventory?

It sounds like you shouldn't be buying any stock goods with credit, right? And there is indeed a case to be made for that point of view. But you can breathe easier – there actually are circumstances under which credit purchase is permissible: non-recourse vendor credit.

Frequently, a vendor (manufacturer, wholesaler, importer) wants to move boxes quickly – and/or believes you are in a position to sell a lot of that stuff. In those cases, many vendors are willing to give you exceptionally good payment terms (which are simply loan terms for the amount of the bill), such as 180 days time-to-pay.

If you encounter such situations, you should do two things:

a) Find buyers for those items. Buyers, that will order them from you and pay before or upon delivery – with a profit margin high enough to pay for most of the rest

b) Negotiate modified payment terms: get the vendor to allow you to return all defect or unsold items at the end of the promotional time for a full credit of their invoiced value. In other words: you want a money-back guarantee on unsold items.

That allows you to move large volumes of product. Since you have started marketing before the products arrived, you can immediately get cash from the shipment (and forward the respective part of the bill to your vendor). So, the whole deal starts producing cash flow right away.

By making partial payments to the vendor, you avoid the trap of (ab)using the cash for anything else but this agreement – and abusing the cash would violate the "what not to use credit for" rules, wouldn't it?

Further, as the vendor sees the payments from your sales coming in, two things happen:

- The payments get reported to business credit agencies – paying 150 days early on a 180-day term is considered great payment discipline and opens further doors for you
- The Vendor sees his risk shrinking as your sales proceed – and that makes it likely you will be considered for the next special deal even while the current one is still not fully sold and paid.

In addition to those, chances are the vendor would extend the loan terms at the end, in case there are still some items left and not yet sold. The vendor's risk has gotten very low at that time, and the logical thing to do is: keep the retailer (you) happy and extend the terms.

But how to get the Business off the ground?

Start small. Very small. But aim at big. It really is that easy.

If you find yourself believing "I just need more money to solve that problem" – then keep in mind: the more money you have, the larger the situation gets. And if you are losing money when you have very little, then throwing more capital at it simply means you will be **losing much more** money. The end of this process is called "bankruptcy".

I once had a friend who dabbled in computer sales while being a full-time university student. When I (carefully, but apparently not careful enough) tried to point out that he was losing money at the prices he was asking, he told me: "I know, I am losing about 15 bucks on each computer. So, I need to sell more of those, then I will make a nice profit."

No, that wasn't supposed to be a joke. Rather, it's a sign of the self-delusion most small business owners succumb to.

Back to your funding problems. The obvious steps for getting cash are:

- Carefully look at your W-2 and your current pay stubs. Is there a sizeable federal income tax withholding amount? That's money you should consider taking control of (yes, you can. If you can't wrap your head around that, ask an accountant – or get in touch with me; I will not give tax advice, but I will be happy to have a brief conversation about the basics of income calculation)
- Are you currently losing cash to existing loans like car loan, 401k loan or credit card?
- Are you currently making payments to a retirement plan? And do you believe those retirement plan investments will yield more than your own business? (If so, stop here and don't start your own business. Seriously.)
- If you are married and you two are filing a joint tax return – check for the same things with your spouse as well
- Where are you spending your money currently? Have an especially careful look at recurring expenses (cell phone, cable or sat tv, club dues, electric bill, internet, but also the daily Starbucks injection); list those items and amounts.

For the points mentioned above, I frequently see the monthly available amounts improve by a few hundred to a few thousand dollars. That's how you get the start funds for your business.

If you want to know how others are handling this need for capital when they actually don't have any – stop by my website and look around (you can find my author's page at the end of the book).

Next step:

Find something which generates a small cash flow. Anything. If that means you have to provide small services – then do it.

Why is that important?

If you cannot sell your small services, you most likely will fail at selling anything larger. Fail now, while it's still free to do so. If you want to run your business, you need to be able to sell.

"Selling", by the way, does not mean "persuading people to buy, just so you shut up." Not at all.

Selling means: you will identify the benefits of what you have to offer, you will identify a need when you see it, and you will be able to explain why your offering does fix the problem and fills the need.

Does this statement mention "price" anywhere?

No, it doesn't. And that's intentional. Because price has no part of the sales process. If you can make a case for your product or service, you will also know its value for your prospective customer. So, you will not overcharge, and you certainly will not give away what you have to offer.

But, the entire sales process is so large that it would blow up this little book in an instant – so, I would like to defer to my other books for that topic. Am I forgiven for doing so?

My FICO score is low... what do I do?

Bad news: you need to learn understanding and handling money and credit. You really do.

Good news: your personal FICO score doesn't matter if you do it the right way.

Don't get me wrong here – if you have bad credit scores, you seriously need to do some homework and clean it up. But that doesn't mean going back and fix everything in your past by paying collection debt that is 6 years old.

That stuff is history, and there is precious little you can do about it. Problems older than 2 years are historical problems – you cannot fix them, as far as FICO is concerned. If you are legally required to deal with it, then do so – but map out a strategy (that's beyond the limits of this book, too).

Your credit score is forward-looking. How likely will you be able and willing to pay your debt due in the next twelve months? Here, your **current** debt comes into play – make sure you handle that properly! (Current debt, unfortunately, also includes all your student loans and any governmental stuff like taxes and speeding tickets from the past. The government makes sure those stay "current debt").

How can you get business credit with a low FICO score? I'm so glad you asked. Because:

Your company can (and should) have its own credit file. Done properly, your business credit doesn't get reported to your personal credit file. Nor does the other way around happen. Simply phrased: you are not your company.

Who are you?

If you open a personal bank account, the bank will ask for your Social Security Number (SSN) – I am sure you can recall that happening. Among other things, they will use this SSN to check your credit file **and** report to that credit file.

If you open a **business bank account**, then you will have to provide the ID number of your business. That's **not** your Social Security Number, though. Instead, your business will have a so-called EIN (originally called employer identification number, but meanwhile it's used as the general business ID for governmental purposes – even when you explicitly stated that you will not employ anybody).

This EIN is the number you will tell the bank when opening the account in the name of the company. Make absolutely sure the business name is spelled **exactly** as it appears on the registration with the state and the IRS. If those two are already slightly different – go back and fix that first. They **must** be absolutely identical.

Then, **on a separate form**, the bank will ask for your personal information because you are the owner – they are legally required to do that. But make absolutely sure the bank account will be opened in the name of the business and with the EIN of the business. On the account setup form, your SSN should appear **nowhere**.

How to get an EIN?

Oh, that's actually very easy. You can go to the IRS website, and most likely the front page will have a button saying "Employer ID number" – click there.

Then, you will get to the EIN page – where you will find a button "Apply for EIN online".

Next, you can fill in the information which you also could provide on form SS-4; but you need to do it either only online or only with the paper form – not both.

Feel free to ask your accountant for help with the EIN application – but in general, it's fairly straightforward.

If you apply online, you will have the EIN usually within a few hours (sent by email to you).

There is, however one tricky aspect:

Some states want you to apply for the EIN **before** you register the LLC. That's no problem – except that the EIN is issued in the **name** of the LLC.

Alas, before you have registered the LLC with the state, you don't really own that name. Now what?

Those states which do require upfront EINs also happen to provide a service to reserve a name for your LLC. So, the real sequence is:

1. Reserve the desired name with the state and see, if it gets approved. If not: choose another one and update the application
2. Once you have the name reserved, apply with the IRS for the soon-to-be-LLC
3. Once you received the EIN, file the organization documents (large words for a piece of paper with the LLCs name & address and your name on it) and provide the required EIN which you just received

That's it – there you have your LLC, freshly baked.

Important:

Don't use words like "The" or "A" at the beginning of your company's name. If you do, it will get messy: the states allow them, but the IRS removes them when assigning the EIN. As a result, your EIN does not match the state documents anymore – and most banks will refuse to open a bank account. My publisher, for example, is commonly referred to as "The Grazing Rock" – but the official company name is only "Grazing Rock LLC". Clearly, somebody was aware of the problem and circumvented it by simply dropping "the" from the official name.

Depending on state and the fees you are willing to pay, the registration process takes anywhere up to 10 days – and probably an additional 10 days to get the certificate from the state back to you. Yeah, you can apply online – but we'll send the response by postal mail anyway...

And now, start memorizing the EIN for your LLC. You will use this one more often than currently your SSN, so you better know it by heart.

From Whence You Came?

Speaking in terms of business credit, you start at nothing. It's probably fair to say that **any** reporting is better than this nothingness on your business credit file.

From here to something, you have several choices:

a) You apply for loans (mainly credit cards) under the EIN, but do guarantee them with your personal SSN

b) You throw some money at some companies known to report to the credit reporting agencies (mainly to Dun & Bradstreet) – and thereby get the reporting agencies to open a credit file for you

c) You figure out what you will be buying for your business **because you need the stuff** and then ask potential vendors: do you guys report to a business credit reporting agency, like Dun & Bradstreet? Then you choose the ones that do – and open an account with them.

Of course, this list misses one major source of credit reporting completely: your bank. As soon as you open a **business** bank account, the bank will report that to a business credit reporting agency. And yes, that's different from personal credit – on the personal side, bank accounts don't get reported unless they involve credit. For businesses, however, the banking relationship **does** get reported. So, you will get your credit file started by merely opening a business bank account.

How Do You Putter Along?

As you are going on with your business, your payment behavior gets recorded and reported to the credit reporting agencies. In this context, it's important to understand a few things.

You can have decent "payment experiences" (that's what your behavior is called) only if you have a choice. So – don't order by credit card. How would you ever prove that you pay on time – if the goods are paid before they are even packaged?

Thus, ask the vendor for payment terms as soon as possible. After a few orders, many will be able to offer you net-30 (means: you have 30 days to pay). Please note: many vendors don't report anything below $50. Make sure your orders are above that amount.

A word of warning: net-30 does **not** mean you should send out the payment on day 30. Net-30 means: on that day, the payment has to be posted to their account and the money has to be available to them. Should you choose to send a check, make sure the check is **in their house** five days **before** the due date.

If you make sure of that, you will get a "satisfactory" business credit rating quickly. However, you can do better.

Just because you have 30 days to pay doesn't mean you can't pay earlier. And that's precisely what you should be doing: if you used the net-30 terms to buffer the time from your customer's payment clearing in your bank account to paying the vendor's bill – then ask your bank how long it will take to "definitely clear". Payments by check are usually clear after 7 days. If you received the payment by PayPal, then it might take two days to get the money from PayPal to your checking account.

Whatever the "cleared-by" date is – on that day the money is definitely available to you, and you can see it posted in your checking account. So, that will be the day when you send out the payment to your vendor. Preferably, the payment should be made by ACH/EFT (electronic funds transfer, which goes directly from bank to bank, rather than check-by-mail).

When your payments arrive substantially before the due date, that will get noticed – and reported. Consistently paying early will push your score up to 12% higher than the normal "satisfactory" experience.

That is what you want!

Why would vendors care to be paid early, when they just gave you 30, 60 or even 90 days to pay?

Because… asking for that time to pay (and then not using it) shows that you are actually planning ahead. You demonstrate that you are in control of your cash flow. Soon, vendors are aware: when you are asking for net-30 terms, that only means "in the worst of all worlds, I may need 30 days"; and when the worst doesn't materialize, they get their money earlier.

You make your LLC into the type of business that vendors and partners **want** to do business with. After a while, your vendors will make you offers like the one mentioned a bit earlier in this book: "Just buy this whole pile of stuff, you have 180 days to pay, and whatever is not sold at that time, you simply return to us." Those offers are no-risk propositions for your LLC.

Why then would a vendor be offering such deals to a customer known for questionable payment discipline, where the vendor would have to be concerned whether he gets paid at all?

He wouldn't.

Where are you going?

After your business credit is established and you have continuous sales, your payment processors (that's whoever accepts payments for you. Can be a credit card processing company, can be PayPal, can be Amazon's payment service) will take notice of the revenue and your credit file. Be consistent about your reliability, and it won't take too long for those payment processors to come up with offers to provide you with cash advances, based on the expected revenues processed by them.

Here, again – be careful what you are using. Use advances only if you essentially already know that certain payments are coming in. That's difficult when you are selling to consumers. But if you are expecting payments from other businesses for ongoing contracts – advances may help protecting your bank balance.

Now, don't run out and spend the money. If the payments don't show up as expected, you need to be able to repay that advance quickly. But for the time being, it can sit in your bank account and make a good impression – especially in case of offers like "the first 20 days of advance at 0% interests".

And the winner is...

Browsing the internet or my mails from startups, I get the impression the highest goal of their business life is an unsecured business credit card with $100K line of credit.

First of all – 100K is not all that much. So, get the fixation on the 100K out of your head.

Second – what are you going to do with that credit card? Your business will have to pay it off within 30 days anyway. And if your business does produce enough cash flow for paying off 100K within in 30 to 60 days, then you may as well wait a few weeks and you have the 100K even without a credit card.

I know, I know, there are tons of reasons for using a business credit card. I agree. But "having 100K" is none of them because - you don't have it.

Last, but not least: do not, I repeat, **do not** believe having a 100K credit line on your credit card would allow you to spend 100K on that card. Much less take 100K as a cash advance.

For more on that topic, see the chapter about business credit cards.

Business Credit Cards

A special kind of animal are the business credit cards. They are familiar – but little do many business owners know about how wrong their beliefs are about the plastic in their wallets...

Credit Cards and Credit Limits

Credit cards come in essentially two versions, and between them is an invisible untold line. That's the line between a subprime credit card and a decent credit card.

Sucker Cards

Subprime cards have, as a matter of principle, a credit limit of less than $5000. If your card falls in that range, you most likely have a subprime card. That tells you how the card company views you – you're a sucker, so to say.

Whether they call it personal card or business credit card – a subprime card is counting on you getting late on payments. It is designed to drain your money via fees and interests as quick as possible – and once you got in there, you will have a very hard time getting out again. That's by design.

And since subprime cards are designed for you to get late on them, you will almost always have to **personally guarantee** your business credit card – which of course means: the limited liability of the LLC or corporation goes out the window; you just signed to be liable for this card.

So, obviously you don't want a subprime card at all. And certainly not for your business.

Decent ("Prime") Cards

A decent business credit card doesn't start below $5000 credit line –even below $7500 is usually out of the question.

For business credit cards, you should expect multiple of $25K as limits – such as 50K, 75K, 100K or the like.

Sky-High?

Speaking of those credit lines on credit cards – a common mistake is to assume you can spend up to that limit. If that's what you think, you are sadly mistaken.

Let me bring some light into the darkness of credit cards:

Those large limits serve a different purpose, which is caused by internal technicalities of credit cards. The amount **really** available to you at any given time is **less than one-third** of the sticker value. But if you want to avoid negative consequences for your business credit file, you absolutely positively **must** stay below one-tenth of the limit. In case of a $100K credit card that means: you cannot charge more than $10K on the card at any given time.

When you're getting close to that number, you need to pay the card balance down again – even before the payment is officially due, and maybe even before you received a monthly statement. But that drill you should know by now... credit lines are not provided to be used. They are a kind of "don't you dare to ever come close", a line in the sand, so to say. That, by the way, is true for personal credit cards as well - unfortunately, most card holders never have been told.

What **can** you do with those large credit card lines, if you can't use them to spend the money?

For one, credit card companies tend to credit the payment amounts right away – even if you made them online. So, if you pay $10K to the card company using their online system, within seconds you have those $10K available to spend on the credit card – even if the balance is updated only nightly.

Think about that for a moment, though. Does the card company actually **know** in this second that your payment will go through and be honored by your bank? No, they don't know that. They surely hope, but they can't be sure.

So – they really are giving you additional credit until the amount is actually handed to them by your bank. That may take a while. The credit card company will feel much better when you are far away from your credit line, so you won't cross it even in the rare event that your payment is not honored by your bank.

Another important reason for large lines of credit are travel expenses. Many merchants are requesting authorization for a much larger amount on your card than you ultimately end up having to pay. Classic examples are hotels and rental car companies. The hotel blocks an amount for "incidentals", means: anything you could charge "to the room" while staying there – the final bill will be charged at the end, and the hotel doesn't want to be left holding the bag in case you don't pay. So, they simply charge a "hold" upfront. And at checkout time, the real bill is charged to the card. Yes, you got that right – **now**, two charges are on the card. The hotel then lets the hold simply expire, so it disappears from your card without a trace. But, for a certain time, you had both charges on there – using up credit line.

Rental car companies are even worse, amount-wise. If your credit card covers CDW (collision damage waiver), then you don't need to buy that insurance from the rental car company. Much to their chagrin, I may add – that's where they would make serious money. But some rental outlets follow the logic "we don't care what will happen afterwards – we will block as much as necessary to cover a collision damage," regardless of whether the card company insures that event anyway.

In case of Budget, for example, even for a subcompact car the hold on the credit card was $3000 when I rented a car earlier this year. The rental fee, by the way, was only about $150.

The credit card insured me against collision damages – so I knew I would never have to pay those $3000. But the rental car company locked that amount with a "hold". And now you can immediately see what those large credit lines are for:

I did spend $150; so, temporarily, this $150 transaction blocked out $3150. Afterwards, it took some days until the hold was released. If I would have had extensive travel plans and rented another car the next day at my next travel destination, Budget's hold would still have been on there. The new hold from the next rental car company would have simply added to the usage of the credit line. And again, the real spending would have been about the same amount ($150), while the frozen "hold" would have reached $6000 combined. Keep in mind – we are talking about a subcompact car (advisable in European cities). The larger the car, the larger the hold used as "security deposit".

By the way, I have had rental car companies which didn't bother to remove the hold – they let it expire after 28 days. Those were 28 days with an impaired line of credit.

To Budget's honor, I have to say: it appears this rental car company is actively removing the hold once the car is checked for damages after you return the car, so you are facing only a few additional days with this amount on hold.

That's why you need business credit cards with large credit lines – otherwise, traveling to several places and renting cars will blow up your credit card in the blink of an eye. For a total charge of maybe $600…

Card-enabled gas pumps do the same – they first charge usually $100, and then they allow you to get gas. Once you're done, it takes them some days to "true up" the amount. Meanwhile, the additional amounts use up your credit line.

In the world of business, things can go fast. Lots of such "temporary" charges can easily lock you up, if you have a card featuring only a token credit line.

So, to answer the question what large credit lines are for: they are **not** for your spending.

They do, however, enable you to **show** that you **could spend** that much.

Why you should NEVER get a credit card with personal guarantee

Sometimes, it feels like a drag, having to wait for all the small startup vendor trade lines to get through and be reported to the reporting agencies – before you can get your first really sizeable unsecured credit card (you know, the normal Master, Visa or AmEx business credit cards).

The temptation is huge to simply go ahead and provide the credit card company with your personal SSN for the business credit card – that way, you can get it much faster.

True – faster.

But that's about the only benefit for doing so. I did mention some problems already before

- As this credit line grows and is used, it will destroy your personal credit. Not to mention the fact that merely applying for a business credit card will hit your credit file as a "hard inquiry" because you are personally guaranteeing it
- As the credit needs of your business are growing, your credit card company will not go that path with you – this card is essentially based on your personal credit. This personal credit doesn't grow with your company

One more problem I didn't point out before, but I feel it's important:

You created the LLC in order to limit your liability – right?

Now you can't wait and co-sign for the business credit card in order to rush the process. Just for this one card, to get started.

What do you think other lenders will see when reviewing your business credit file? They will see: you registered the LLC, and just two months later you had your first business credit card, at a time when you barely had 5 agency-reporting trade lines with vendors, establishing your credit file.

How stupid do you think they are? **Of course** they can immediately conclude what that means: the guy has personally guaranteed the credit card. **Fantastic** – so we as new lenders will require a personal guarantee, too!

And so it goes… you will never be able to get out of personal guarantees for this LLC. Then what's the point, really?

Bank Loans

Banks come into mind as first source of credit. In reality, they are about the last one. Businesses are inherently risky unless you understand them very well. Most bankers are not bankers because they understand businesses.

In other words: a bank will base their decision on something even a banker understands. (If you are a competent banker, I need apologize – I know there are many serious and professional bank specialist, who are knowledgeable, competent and helpful. But you know as well as I do that there are also uncountable armies of ignorant "is it already 5pm" type guys. What are the probabilities of my readers finding a competent commercial banker, compared to the odds of falling into the hands of one of those other guys?)

What could banks therefore be looking at, when it comes to making a credit decision? Easy: it's your account balance.

As a rule of thumb: unless the recent 90 days before your loan application did show an ongoing **minimum** account balance of $10,000 – don't bother to apply.

Having $10K in your account at all times just barely gets you into being considered for a loan.

Sure, you could offer a personal guarantee. But – and that is what you need to tell your bank as well – there's a problem with personal guarantees: if the bank uses your personal finances as base for the credit decisions (which is the case, if you guarantee it), then it's just a question of a few months until your business outgrows your ability to guarantee its loans without ruining your own credit.

Keep in mind: personal lines of credit must have a reasonable relationship to your **income** – because that's what you can use to repay them. **Business** lines of credit must have a reasonable relationship to your **turnover** – which is the total sales price of everything you are selling. You can use that amount to pay off the credit lines simply because you used them to pay for the items in the first place.

Using your personal credit (based on income) to back a loan which is used for revenue, that's just a total magnitude mismatch. And doomed to fail very soon, since hopefully your company's revenue is growing much faster than your personal income.

Other Lenders

When you need more flexibility than banks can offer, you may need to look to alternative lenders. Those are lenders specialized on specific aspects of your business – for which they are able to quickly determine an amount they can loan you for that aspect.

Earlier, I did mention the payment processors which oftentimes extend credit to you, based on their expectations of future sales revenue processed by them. If everything turns out as they predict, you won't be paying them "back" – instead, they just take their loan payoffs from your future revenue.

Other lenders do cash flow financing – they look at your bank account and your accounting information, determine how much free cash flow your business can produce and how much therefore you can pay back using that cash flow.

Many lenders go for asset backing – that means: you hand over an asset as collateral for the loan. The best-known case is real estate, and the collateralized loan is called the mortgage loan. When you buy a personal home with a bank loan, the bank holds the mortgage to the home – that's an asset-backed loan: if you default on your loan, the bank owns the real estate. The same holds true with any other asset-backed lending. Whatever is pledged as collateral – if you don't pay as agreed, you lose this asset.

A special case of asset-backed loans are loans against your accounts receivable. Whenever you are sending out an invoice, you are considered to have a receivable – and, sooner or later, it is assumed that you will be paid this amount.

After your business has been going on for a while, you will have a reasonable number of experiences with invoices in the past, so lenders can make a reasonable judgement about how many of your invoices (and which amount) actually will be paid. With this knowledge, they can use your receivables as collateral for a loan provided to you. Mostly, the lenders are doing the billing and collecting as well (just to make sure they get the money, I assume).

This type of financing is available as "accounts receivable financing" (if the buyer fails to pay, you are still on the hook for the loan) or as "factoring", in which case the risk of your buyer defaulting on the invoice is somebody else's problem.

Hint: Factoring is more expensive than account receivable financing – simply because the lender has to bite potential losses. But do not assume you would get away unscathed: if your factoring partner is losing money on your invoices, the terms for the next round of factoring will worsen. In other words: you will be paying for the loss over time.

There are tons of other financing options available to a well-documented business. As a basic rule: if you cannot tell where the business' cash is coming from, where it is going, and in which time frames what will happen – chances are, cash won't be coming from anywhere. Certainly not from lenders.

There is still a lot to be said about business credit – if you want to know more, get in touch. At the time of this writing, the topic of business credit is planned to fill an entire book. I'll be happy to keep you updated when it's available!

Recordkeeping

One of your most important tasks in your business is recordkeeping. Unfortunately, it's usually also a quite neglected task.

While almost everybody seems to immediately agree on how important recordkeeping is – very few small businesses actually follow through on it. Why is that?

Records Reality: No Clue

The reality is, most small business owners have no clue what recordkeeping really requires. Yeah, sure – records need to be kept. Somehow. That's how the accountants end up with a shoe box full of receipts in February of the next year.

I'm probably not disclosing much of a secret by telling you: this "method" is not going to work for you.

Since we're at it, we may as well go through the obvious questions you may have when it comes to recordkeeping:

- What are records, really?
- What is their purpose – and are there formal requirements?
- Is recordkeeping the same as accounting?
- Which way do I sort the records?

What are records?

Records are all documents which represent a financial transaction, be it past, present or future.

That seems quite vague, doesn't it? Let me explain:

If you receive spam mail and trash it right away, obviously this did not pertain to any financial transaction – neither in the past nor in the future nor in the present. So, this doesn't belong to your records.

If you order a printer from an online web site for your business – that clearly already does or very soon will lead to a payment and a shipment of goods to you. That makes it a financial transaction – so the order does belong to the company's records. Yes, **the order** – not just the invoice!

When the printer is delivered, it comes with a packing slip or other shipping document. You need to check this document for accuracy and confirm that you have received what it says you should receive. This, too, belongs to the transaction – and therefore to your records.

Either included in the package or by separate mail or email, you will receive the invoice, detailing the charges and showing the method of payment used or to be used.

That, too, is part of the financial transaction – so it goes to your records as well.

There is a separate Thank-You letter enclosed with the invoice with nothing more on it than just some text telling you how pleasant you are as a customer? No, that's not part of a financial transaction. You don't need to keep this thing.

If you need to pay your phone bill (which belongs to your records), you may send a check. Now, let me ask – how does anyone know which check has been sent and what exactly was written on that check? For all we know, you could have used a company check to pay for your personal phone bill, right? So – how can you document what you wrote on that check? You guessed it: scan or copy the check before you send it out! The copy goes into your records!

On the day the check gets sent, you enter that fact onto a list. This list will show the dates, recipients and contents of mail that your company did send out – and therefore serve as ledger for outgoing mail and packages. If you send something registered or with tracking services, you can enter the tracking information in this list as well.

This "outgoing mail" list is part of your records. That way, you can easily retrieve the information about a document or check having been sent. That's valuable, especially when dealing with recipients who routinely drop the ball somewhere (government agencies come to mind).

Your company's bank statements are records, as well as your company's credit card statements.

Whenever you use a company credit card, or when you are paying with your personal card on behalf of the company – you will need to keep that receipt with your company records. It's a part of the payment process, so it indeed does constitute a financial transaction.

What is their purpose?

You should know that human memory is chronically unreliable, especially when it comes to long sequences of transactions. Despite what you may think – only three transactions per day for one week are sufficient to overload our mental capacity. And we shall hope that you will have to work on more than three transactions per day!

Recognizing this fact, the law requires you to keep records in a form which is readable by others. For a long time, that meant: on paper. Meanwhile, for most cases electronic storage is permissible as well – but caution: **you** are responsible for the ability to retrieve stored data after, say, four years. "The USB stick lost its memory" is no excuse – as a diligent business owner, you should know that flash memory is **not** durable at all, and therefore not suited to comply with recordkeeping requirements. Nor are magnetic hard drives, by the way. Maybe paper records are not the worst option, after all.

Your records will be needed whenever, at some time in the future, you must be able to prove that you did do something or didn't do something. If you have the records to show (or not show) something, then the burden of proof falls on your opponent – and that opponent then must come up with something better than your records. Which by tendency is difficult – well-kept records have quite some standing power in court.

Typical cases are:

- IRS audits: when the IRS questions a business expense or claims you "forgot" to include certain income – refer to your records and show that such additional income doesn't show up anywhere. And the claimed expense was recorded in the company's books all along, together with any payment related to this expense.

- Legal cases: an attacking attorney usually tries to remove your LLC's liability protection by claiming you didn't treat the LLC as separate from yourself. If you can show that you indeed did treat the LLC as an own entity **and** that you made sure all business activity was responsible under the circumstances – then the attacking attorney will have to prove you wrong. **If, however,** you don't have the records to show all that – then the attacker essentially has already won his case against you.

- When you have sold gift certificates and your records allow you to track which certificate has been given out, when it was redeemed, for what and by whom – then it will be difficult for tricksters to redeem the same gift certificate twice. Attempts to redeem the same certificate several times are way more common than you may think. If you cannot prove that the certificate has already been redeemed, you are doomed to lose a lot of money

- If a vendor sends you a long list of invoices, claiming that some of those haven't been paid by you – can you prove him wrong, or will you have to pay again even if you did already pay? With proper records, you can immediately not only tell **that** you paid, but also **when** and **how**. And, if you sent a check, you also will be able to tell the vendor when and at which bank they cashed your check. That, dear reader, is **"proof of payment"**. Not just "I think I did pay". Again, these cases are more common than you may think – especially in companies with more than just the owner doing the work, it's not uncommon that employees make mistakes when entering the data, so your payment gets credited to somebody else's account with that vendor.

In short, the records serve as a reliable memory for your company. The reliable memory that we humans don't have.

Is recordkeeping the same as accounting?

The two are closely related – but they are not the same. Accounting is a certain system used for recording financials, while recordkeeping is the system used to store and retrieve the actual documents.

Obviously, you can account only for what exists – so every accounting entry is based on some kind of record. But you can very well have records which don't trigger an accounting entry. Let's think of an offer you are making to a customer – a certain product on a certain date for a certain price. Until the offer expired or the customer ordered, you don't even know whether this offer will turn into a transaction. But you should make sure you keep it as a record – otherwise you wouldn't know what you did offer!

Which way do I sort the records?

In current times, the best way is: chronologically. So, you just file every document as it comes in. When looking up the papers, you know exactly: as you go through them, you are going back in time. Rather than jumping around.

Additionally, you will have scanned and archived all records – and your computer will easily be able to sort and search by whatever your heart's desire may be in any moment. Once the computer has located the document electronically, you can still go back and retrieve the paper version – because now you know its date, so it's easy to find.

Suggestion:

Assign record numbers to each document. You can do that by hand, or you can buy a stamp which automatically counts the number upwards. That way, it's faster to find records without any doubts – the number is unique.

Such a unique number makes it easy for the accountant to supplement the accounting entry with a reference to the record which caused that entry. Again, that saves you from having to compare all accounting entries for a transaction with the actual paper – very helpful if you have multiple similar transactions on the same date and need to find out which accounting entry refers to what document.

And how do I "keep" the records?

Sounds easy – but sticking to it is a challenge. Do this:

No later than **every evening**, get all documents, receipts, invoices and whatever belongs to your records – and follow those easy steps:

1. Get them to letter size. If the paper is already letter-sized, then you skip this step. In all other cases, glue the receipt (or whatever it is) to a letter-sized sheet of paper. **Note:** If the receipt has important information on the back side, you cannot glue the back side to anything. Affix the receipt with tape instead – so you can flip the receipt over like a page in a book
2. Write today's date in the upper right corner, preferably above anything else. This assures that you can find the date in less than one second – without first reading half of the page to find out where the date is printed
3. Below the date, place your record number as mentioned in the previous subchapter. Each record number should be used only once!
4. Scan the entire page and store the file in your digital archive
5. Punch holes in the (now) letter-size document
6. File it in a 3-ring binder in top position. So, the newest records will be on top.

It's not all that difficult, is it? Yet, among ten small businesses, maybe two are following any system at all.

These 3-ring binders, you will hand to your accountant in regular intervals (preferably weekly, but definitely not further spaced out than monthly). The accountant then will do his accounting magic, and you still have the electronic archive to fall back on while the records are with the accountant. Neat, isn't it?

Electronic Archive...?

Oh, right – don't make it appear more complex than it is. Yes, there is software in the market which does handle recordkeeping and document storage in wonderful ways. The price tags, however, are commonly less wonderful.

Here's a trick you can use for starters:

Since you are keeping records officially on paper, your electronic records do not need to follow the strict rules otherwise imposed. The electronic records are essentially for your internal use only.

That allows you to use a really simple solution:

Whenever you have scanned a document, change its name to reflect the current date (YYYY-MM-DD) and describe the content of the scan. For example, a file name for an invoice might look like

2018-02-14 Flowerworld Invoice 234232.pdf

Just reading this file name already tells you what to expect – that saves work later. Writing the date in exactly the way I suggest (YYYY-MM-DD) results in the files being sorted by date (when you simply request "sort by name", you will automatically get a date-sorted record list). No additional software required.

Finally, you just move the newly scanned and renamed files to a folder on your computer where you keep the records – and there you have your electronic archive.

If afterwards you need to find Invoice 234232, which Flowerworld claims to be of a different amount than you ultimately paid: simply ask your computer to search for that invoice. Inevitably, that file will show up – and you can easily have a look and determine what the original invoice really said.

The End

If you have made it here without skipping half of the book, then you should know more about the topic of LLCs than most of your fellow Americans. Even more than many who actually **did** form an LLC or Corporation in the past (oftentimes both because they didn't know better).

That means, at this point you have the foundation to make informed decisions and to get into the really juicy stuff with your accountant and attorney.

You know what to look out for, and you know what you shouldn't do when it comes to bootstrapping your brand-new LLC.

I would like to invite you to share your experiences, questions and frustrations with others just like you. Visit my facebook site (see next page in this book) and send me a message!

And now – bark like a big dog!

About the Author

S. Ralf Carter is self-employed and business owner since more than 30 years; about half of this time, he has been performing diverse functions exclusively in the software industry.

Wherever there has been the opportunity to try wrong decisions, Ralf Carter most likely did try them or at least experienced first-hand how business partners had to work through the consequences of their own suboptimal decisions.

During the second half of his career, Ralf Carter additionally provided (and still does provide) his experience for the training of entrepreneurs and business start-ups.

Born in Germany, over time he has called several parts of the world his home. Right now, a sunny Mediterranean island is his residence of choice.

You can get in touch in English or German language via his facebook page at

> https://www.facebook.com/SRalfCarter

or by email:

> ralfC@grazingrock.com

www.ingramcontent.com/pod-product-compliance
Lightning Source LLC
Chambersburg PA
CBHW051329220526
45468CB00004B/1556